This book is dedicated to our angel that watches over us,

Kaden Miles Britton

When I go to sleep at night

I think about what I want

to become in life.

I dream about what seeds

I need to sow

To help me on the way as I grow.

I must plant seeds of high self-esteem, good manners,

and integrity.

These seeds will help me grow into a strong and

responsible adult.

There are so many ideas and several careers that will allow me to be a superhero to others, both far and near.

I can explore the World and make big changes, but with so many possibilities, it's so hard to choose!

I can imagine myself as anything, because I know that I can become anything that I want to be, as long as I always believe in me!

When I grow up I can be an astronaut, and study the sun, moon, and stars!

I can also be an engineer and design fancy cars. Or I can be a doctor and perform surgeries, I will help others get well and heal from injuries.

Maybe I can be a CEO of a business, and provide jobs for others or I can become an animator and create cool cartoon movies like Disney.

When I grow up I can be an architect, and design cool buildings, like I do with my legos or I can be an artist, and draw beautiful pictures for the World to see.

Maybe I will be a teacher and nurture kids like you

and me!

I believe that I can be anything that I want to be as

long as I believe in me!

There are so many careers for me to explore indeed, and I will continue to imagine about them and keep them in my dreams.

I will work hard in school, and keep good grades.

Because I know that one day I will go to college, and

it is only for the brave.

There are so many things I want to see when I grow up. I will continue to sow good seeds so that my dreams and I will continue to grow.

Since I have plenty of time before I grow up, I will

explore all of my options, and learn all that I need to

know.

Whatever life brings, I will remember this one thing.

I can be whatever I want to be as long as I believe in me!